TIMELINE OF FRÉDÉRIC CHOPIN'S LIFE

1810 Frédéric Chopin is born in Żelazowa Wola, Poland. Later that year, the Chopin family moves to Warsaw.

1817 Frédéric shows an interest in music. He begins piano lessons and composes his first work, Polonaise in G Minor.

1818 Seven-year-old Frédéric gives his first public concert.

1822 Frédéric begins taking piano lessons from Joseph Elsner, one of the best music teachers in Poland.

1824 While on vacation in the countryside, Frédéric hears Polish folk music for the first time. It inspires him and influences his music for the rest of his life.

1825 Frédéric plays for Czar Alexander I, the powerful ruler of Russia.

1830 Chopin leaves Poland forever. He travels to Vienna and then Paris. Both cities are filled with people who appreciate music and welcome musicians and composers.

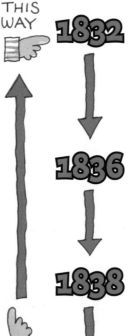
THIS WAY

UP HERE

1832 Chopin gives his first concert in Paris. Wealthy music lovers think his music is great. Frédéric continues writing new pieces and becomes a popular piano teacher.

1836 Chopin goes to Germany, where he meets some of the world's greatest composers, including Felix Mendelssohn and Robert Schumann.

1838 Frédéric falls in love with Aurore Dupin, better known as George Sand. Frédéric starts to become seriously ill with a lung disease.

1839 -1847 Despite poor health, Chopin keeps composing, performing, and teaching.

1848 Chopin performs in England and Scotland. When he becomes too sick to go on, he returns to Paris.

1849 At the age of 39, Frédéric Chopin dies peacefully in his apartment in Paris, France.

GETTING TO KNOW
THE WORLD'S
GREATEST COMPOSERS

F R E D E R I C
CHOPIN

WRITTEN AND ILLUSTRATED BY MIKE VENEZIA

CONSULTANT
DONALD FREUND, PROFESSOR OF COMPOSITION
INDIANA UNIVERSITY SCHOOL OF MUSIC

CHILDREN'S PRESS®

An Imprint of Scholastic Inc.

To Mary Wong, a special friend!

Picture Acknowledgements
Photographs ©: Archives of the Chopin Society: 10, 13; Art Resource, NY: 28 top (Lauros-Giraudon/Musee de la Ville de Paris, Musee Carnavalet), 3, 14 (Giraudon), 6 (Scala), 11 (Tate Gallery); Bridgeman Art Library International Ltd., London/New York: 16, 17 (PFA107919 *The Midday Rest* by Franciszek Streitt, oil on panel/Phillips, The International Fine Art Auctioneers, UK.); Corbis-Bettmann: 32; Gamma-Liaison, Inc.: 31 top (Hulton Getty); Mary Evans Picture Library: 28 bottom (Explorer), 18 (Steve Rumney), 23, 31 bottom.

Colorist for interior illustrations: Kathy Hickey

Library of Congress Cataloging-in-Publication Data

Names: Venezia, Mike, author, illustrator.
Title: Frederic Chopin / written and illustrated by Mike Venezia.
Description: Revised edition. | New York : Children's Press, 2017. | Series:
   Getting to know the world's greatest composers | Includes index.
Identifiers: LCCN 2017022724 | ISBN 9780531226575 (library binding) | ISBN
   9780531230350 (pbk.)
Subjects: LCSH: Chopin, Fr?ed?eric, 1810-1849--Juvenile literature. |
   Composers--Biography--Juvenile literature.
Classification: LCC ML3930.C46 V45 2017 | DDC 786.2092 [B] --dc23 LC record
   available at https://lccn.loc.gov/2017022724

©2018 by Mike Venezia Inc.

All rights reserved. Published in 2018 by Children's Press, an imprint of Scholastic Inc.
Printed in United States of America 113

SCHOLASTIC, CHILDREN'S PRESS, and associated logos are trademarks and/or registered trademarks of Scholastic Inc., 557 Broadway, New York, NY 10012.

1 2 3 4 5 6 7 8 9 10 R 27 26 25 24 23 22 21 20 19 18

Portrait of Chopin, by Eugène Delacroix

Frédéric Chopin was born in 1810 in Żelazowa Wola, Poland. Almost all of his compositions were written just for the piano. Chopin wrote beautiful music for the piano and invented new ways of playing it.

Frédéric Chopin loved and understood music at a very early age. When he was about four years old, he liked to lie under the piano while his older sister, Louise, practiced. Sometimes he would burst into tears because he thought the music was so beautiful.

Wolfgang Amadeus Mozart

Frédéric soon began experimenting with the piano himself. His parents were amazed by how quickly their son learned things on his own.

When Frédéric was six years old, his parents decided to find him a teacher. Adalbert Zywny was Frédéric's first music teacher. He taught his new student basic piano skills. He also taught Frédéric a love for the music of such great composers from the past as Johann Sebastian Bach and Wolfgang Amadeus Mozart.

It wasn't long before everyone realized that young Frédéric Chopin had a remarkable gift for music. Frédéric once told his father that it would be much easier for him to express his feelings if they could be put into musical notes.

Frédéric Chopin was a good student and listened to his teacher. But he enjoyed making up his own music more than anything else.

By the time Chopin was eight years old, some of his musical pieces had been published, and he had even given a public concert. At the concert, Frédéric was more worried about what the audience thought of his new velvet coat and collar than what they

thought about his music. As it turned out, the audience loved Chopin's music.

Frédéric's parents, Justine and Nicolas Chopin

Mr. and Mrs. Chopin were proud of Frédéric's musical talent. They made sure he had an excellent education in other areas, too. Mr. Chopin taught French to the children of wealthy families in Warsaw, Poland's capital city. He knew the importance of education and good manners.

The Chopins became friends with many of Warsaw's most interesting people. Frédéric got used to having dukes, countesses, poets, authors, and artists visiting his home all the time.

Frédéric at the piano as a young boy

While growing up, Frédéric Chopin was always polite, well mannered, and concerned about dressing neatly. Because of this, some people think he must have had a boring childhood. But Frédéric was like lots of other kids. One of his favorite things to do was ride horses, although he later wrote that he wasn't very good at it.

Cartoons drawn by
Frédéric as a young boy

He also had a
good sense of humor.
Frédéric drew funny
pictures of his teachers,
schoolmates, and friends
that kept everyone
laughing. He like ice-
skating, and he had lots
of girlfriends, too.

Poland was having all kinds of problems when Frédéric Chopin was growing up. The biggest problem was that Poland was always being taken over by more powerful countries. One of Poland's neighbors, Russia, decided it would like to keep part of Poland for itself.

When Frédéric was fifteen years old, he was asked to give a performance for Czar Alexander I, the ruler of Russia. The czar gave Frédéric a diamond ring after the concert. That was an exciting moment for Frédéric Chopin.

Czar Alexander I of Russia

Chopin was becoming well known and appreciated. But he was also becoming bothered that the Polish people were being bossed around by outsiders.

Chopin's teenage years were very important. He was getting his ideas together on how he felt about his country, his music, and his future. He especially learned a lot from going on summer vacations with his family. In the countryside of Poland,

The Midday Rest, a painting by Franciszek Streitt showing the Polish countryside in the 1800s

Frédéric Chopin saw the hardworking Polish peasants and heard their music.

People had been singing and dancing to this music for hundreds of years. Frédéric got lots of ideas for his own music from these trips.

One popular folk dance Frédéric learned about was the mazurka. The music for this dance can be lively and exciting or sweetly sad. It was an important part of the lives of Polish peasants. People felt proud of their homeland when they heard and danced mazurkas. They knew they had something of their own that even a bossy czar couldn't take from them.

Eastern European folk dancing

Frédéric Chopin ended up composing more than fifty of his own mazurkas. He added his own special touches, and mazurkas became some of his most popular works. Chopin's Mazurka in B-flat Major, Op.7, No.1, is a good example of how he captured the spirit, fun, and excitement of Polish life in his music.

After Frédéric finished high school and music college, he traveled to other countries in Europe to give performances. After a few very successful trips, Frédéric and his family and teachers thought there would be better opportunities for him in cities like Vienna, Austria; and Paris, France. Music was much more popular in these cities than it was in Warsaw.

On November 2, 1830, Frédéric Chopin decided to leave Poland to make his fortune. He didn't know it then, but he would never return to the country he loved so much.

At the time Chopin left home, Poland wasn't the only country with problems. People all over Europe were getting fed up with outside governments trying to take over their countries or having their own uncaring rulers run their lives. It was a dangerous time to be traveling.

Even so, Frédéric continued on to Paris. Along the way, he heard shocking news. A group of Polish citizens had started a rebellion to throw out the Russian czar and his soldiers. Frédéric was upset, and was worried about the safety of his friends and family.

Street fighting in Warsaw, Poland, during the 1830 revolt against Russian rule

He became inspired to compose one of his most exciting and powerful pieces, the Étude in C Minor (also known as the "Revolutionary Étude.") This piece is filled with the spirit of rebellion. In parts, it seems to explode with rushing piano sounds! All of Chopin's hopes for his country come alive in this amazing piano piece.

When Frédéric Chopin arrived in Paris, he couldn't believe how busy and exciting the city was. Paris was filled with famous authors, poets, and artists—and especially musicians and composers. Frédéric was welcomed right away. He became best friends with one of the most famous pianists of all time, Franz Liszt.

Liszt was a piano virtuoso. A virtuoso is a person who does something better than almost anyone else in the world. Chopin was surprised to find out that virtuosos would sometimes challenge each other to see who was the best. Audiences loved these contests. Once Frédéric watched Liszt and another virtuoso have a play-off.

In the past, Frédéric had given concerts as a way of making money and becoming better known. But even though he was one of the best pianists ever, Chopin never really enjoyed playing for big audiences. In fact, he was usually terrified of performing!

In Paris, people weren't that interested in Chopin's concerts because Chopin wasn't as big a show-off and didn't play as loudly as other piano virtuosos. That was just fine with Frédéric. Now he was able to spend more time

composing and playing for small groups of friends. Chopin also found he could make lots of money giving piano lessons to members of the wealthy families he met in Paris.

George Sand dressed in men's clothing

One evening, when Frédéric was at a party, Franz Liszt introduced him to an unusual woman author named George Sand. George Sand's books were very popular at the time. They were filled with new ideas and different ways of looking at life. George sometimes dressed in men's clothes and smoked cigars, something women didn't really do at that time.

George Sand smoking a cigar while watching Franz Liszt play the piano

At first, Frédéric thought George was a
little strange, but after he got to know her,
he fell deeply in love. For the next ten years,
Frédéric Chopin and George Sand had one
of the most famous romances of the century.
It was during these years that Chopin
composed most of his greatest works.

*C*hopin composed so many different types of music that it's sometimes hard to keep them all straight. Some of his most popular pieces are dances, like mazurkas, polonaises, and waltzes. Most of these pieces weren't really meant to be danced to. They were more about the spirit of dancing and the excitement of the times. He also wrote études. These are short studies used for teaching piano. But Chopin turned them into much more than simple studies. In the "Revolutionary Étude," for example, you can almost feel Chopin's fiery temper. Chopin's Waltz in D-flat Major, Op.64, No.1, is so quick and breathless that everyone calls it the "Minute Waltz" (although it's almost impossible to play it in a minute!).

Chopin's piano

The nocturnes are another popular category. The word *nocturne* means "night piece." Chopin's nocturnes are slow and dreamy in feeling. They're great to listen to when you want to relax and just think about things.

Chopin composing music

Frédéric Chopin in 1849

*U*nfortunately, Frédéric Chopin had poor health for most of his life. When he and George Sand broke up, he slowly became worse. Chopin wrote a few more pieces and gave some concerts until he felt too weak to do any more. He died quietly in Paris in 1849.

No matter which category of his music they listen to, most people find Frédéric Chopin's compositions to be some of the most original, sensitive, and beautiful music ever.

LEARN MORE BY TAKING THE
CHOPIN QUIZ!

(ANSWERS ON THE NEXT PAGE.)

1. One of Chopin's most famous piano pieces, Waltz in D-flat Major, is also known as the "Minute Waltz." But that's not its only nickname. What is the other fun name for this quick-paced waltz?
- **a** "The Pierogi Waltz"
- **b** "The Oh, no! I'm Late for My Dental Appointment Waltz"
- **c** "The Little Dog Waltz"

2. TRUE OR FALSE: Chopin is best known for his piano pieces, but he also wrote lots of music that featured the oboe, tuba, harp, and violin.

3. When Frédéric Chopin left Poland to make his way to the famous music cities of Europe, his friends gave him a very special gift. What did Frédéric find when he opened the gift?
- **a** Chocolate brownies
- **b** Dirt
- **c** Exercise equipment

4. TRUE OR FALSE: Before he began a piano performance, Chopin would often insist on playing in total darkness.

5. Aside from the piano, what other instrument was Chopin an expert at playing?
- **a** Trombone
- **b** Peruvian bone flute
- **c** Organ

6. TRUE OR FALSE: Frédéric Chopin performed only thirty public concerts during his life.

7. Frédéric Chopin made a living by publishing his music and playing the piano. What else did he do to make money?
- **a** He started a successful chain of fast-food Polish sausage restaurants
- **b** He gave hourly piano lessons
- **c** He was an Uber carriage driver

ANSWERS

1. **c** One evening, Chopin's girlfriend, George Sand, said she wished she had the talent to write a waltz for her frisky little dog who was always running around chasing its tail. George's wish inspired Chopin to sit down at the piano and compose the famous waltz on the spot!

2. **FALSE** Just about all of Chopin's 250 music pieces were written for solo piano. He did write a few pieces that included other instruments, but those compositions always featured the piano.

3. **b** Chopin's friends gave him a container of Polish soil. It was something he always kept to remind him of the country he loved so much. When Frédéric died in Paris, the soil was sprinkled on his coffin.

4. **TRUE** Chopin felt his listeners would enjoy and "feel" his music better if they listened to it in complete darkness. It's fun to try. When you listen to a beautiful Chopin piece in the dark, it can become a magical music experience.

5. **c** Frédéric Chopin received organ lessons as a teenager and gave recitals in Warsaw. Later on, he would play the organ, but only on rare occasions.

6. **TRUE** Frédéric Chopin always hated playing in front of large audiences. Though known all over the world for his music, he gave only about thirty public concerts during his life. Frédéric much preferred playing at home for his friends or at small social gatherings.

7. **b** People all over Paris wanted to take piano lessons from Frédéric Chopin. He was able to charge lots of money teaching wealthy people to play the piano.